Blokelore and Blokesongs

Blokelore and Blokesongs

from

Old Fred

(Fred Faraday, Philosopher)

as recorded by

Robert Conquest

WAYWISER

First published in 2012 by

THE WAYWISER PRESS

Bench House, 82 London Road, Chipping Norton, Oxon OX7 5FN, UK
P.O. Box 6205, Baltimore, MD 21206, USA
http://waywiser-press.com

Editor-in-Chief
Philip Hoy

Senior American Editor
Joseph Harrison

Associate Editors
Eric McHenry Clive Watkins Greg Williamson

A CIP catalogue record for this book is available from the British Library

ISBN 978-1-904130-48-2

Printed and bound by
T.J. International Ltd., Padstow, Cornwall, PL28 8RW

Dedicated, with permission,

to

Wendy Cope and Lachlan Mackinnon

The high tribunal of these two
Faults those omitting Fred
From status in (as is his due)
Our culture's A to Zed.

Acknowledgements

Some of these poems first appeared in *The Listener, Light Quarterly*, *Standpoint* and the *New Criterion*.

Contents

Contents

BARE ESSENTIALS

Fred Meditates on Nature

Fred's always envied butterflies
   Not for their sips and flits,
But the unfair advantages
   Their life-cycle permits.

At first on fuss and toil intent
   In caterpillar guise;
Then chrysalis retirement;
   And last, the sensuous skies.

And why the human species too
   Aren't programmed just the same
Seems slipshod (though Fred's not sure who,
   Or what, should take the blame):

To get the plodding over first;
   A snooze, and then to fly
Into a crashing sexual burst,
   And go out on a high!

It's not that his own love life's grim –
   Fred just finds nature great
To give philosophers like him
   Footnotes to human fate.

Unfair to Fred

Quite early on Fred noticed it:
  A girl finds that, for her,
A chap behaving like a shit
  Is "showing character",

Or "challenging" the girl to see
  What she can make of him,
While those behaving decently
  Are left out on no limb ...

One girl who dealt Fred blighted love
  Then went and wed the blighter,
Much later came to tell him of
  The spasms of rage and fright a

Glimpse of the sod – by now her ex –
  Induced in her for years;
He'd also been a dud at sex
  – All music to Fred's ears.

A tough kid: now she frankly said
  That with her youthful blooper
She'd dished herself as well as Fred ...
  The honey still looked super.

Things had turned out to validate
  Fred's views in model fashion;
And yet he felt they'd left too late
  A re-run of their passion.

A waste of time, a waste of what
  We don't have too much of,
Fred doesn't think of it a lot:
  But yes, a waste of love.

Fred Forgets

You well may say a long lost girl
    Should now be cased in nacre,
An irritant become the pearl
    Only his mind can make her.

But Fred so seldom thinks of her.
    It's long ago. – And to be
Honest, he would now prefer
    A sapphire or a ruby.

Fred's Fane

Of course Fred's often heard the claim
    That religious ex-
perience is much the same
    (Or *just* the same) as sex.

Fred's known times when, in seconds flat,
    The female form divine'd
Brimmed up so high with mana that
    It nearly blew his mind.

But sometimes bedding down with such
    Turned to a playful game
While one who's not impressed so much
    Fair lit the night with flame ...

Perhaps among the mystics too
    Such paradoxes reign.
Of course, on a more general view
    The parallels are plain.

Fred on Myth

Though Orpheus won the laurel crown
   He drank the bitter cup:
Eurydice first let him down
   Then Maenads tore him up.

An Orpheus Complex? Fred won't fuss
   With such an ancient tale
(Unlike old Freud with Oedipus)
   – The thought, though, turns him pale.

Mere myth? – But that old Greek (thinks Fred)
   Who told the tale as true
Had some material in his head
   On which he later drew.

Fred's Phraseology

"Soft breasts, hard heart". It does sound quite
   A general apophthegm.
Fred meant it only to indict
   One girl, not all of them.

Yet gets the blame when girls find that
   Some bitter chap who'll not
Observe this careful caveat
   Applies it to the lot.

Feckless Fred

Woman's mentality is not
  (Fred holds) clear about man's.
They think us a seducing lot
  Who lay cold-blooded plans.

He takes a girl, say twice, to lunch,
  Then makes a dinner date.
That night, just rolling with the punch
  He might, or might not, wait.

And if he does consider how
  To get her to his flat,
It's only, as they put it now,
  Because that's where it's at.

Chaps may, what's more, fall madly in
  Love, as Fred once did,
His mind short-circuited by gin,
  Committed by his id.

Not Fred's Style

If you are wanting to annoy
  (As Fred hopes that you're not),
Nowadays there's many a ploy
  To make girls' cheeks go hot.

One method Fred has sometimes struck:
  With eyes half-shut and grin
Of patronising homage, chuck
  A girl beneath the chin.

"Well, well, my little one" will serve
  To aggravate your crime;
But even if you have the nerve
  Fred doubts you'll have the time.

Because, meanwhile, the chance is high
  That, when the penny drops
You'll rapidly be silenced by
  A smack across the chops.

Meekness, in fact, has had its day
  (If it was ever found),
But still nostalgia for it may
  Give chaps the runaround.

If so, to realists like Fred
  Their compensation seems
Only attainable in bed
  – That is, of course, in dreams.

One of Fred's Fancies

Fred knows that, in their sexual stint,
   Breasts stand as stimuli
Designed by Nature to imprint
   The male's obsessive eye.

It may be just a whim, but still
   Nature might now, he feels,
Evolve, on the same principle,
   Extensible high heels.

Fred Goes into Detail

Women distinguish many a hue
   Far beyond men's scope:
'Teal' it seems is vaguely blue,
   A muddy shine is 'Taupe'.

"Minutiae from which," we groan,
   "There's little to be learned."
But Fred's not one to leave a stone,
   However small, unturned.

Well yes, we say, the colour sense
   Differs in him and her;
So girls' minds aren't the same as men's?
   Whoever thought they were!

Fred replies that what we've known's
   Been attitudes to love
And shops and time and telephones
   – All superficial stuff,

But now he feels he's found the key:
   Whoever thought a girl'd
Be structured to not even see
   The same objective world?

Yet Fred approves of Nature's plan,
   (From which we can't escape):
Who'd want a woman like a man,
   Merely of different shape?

Fred in a Muddle

Though lots more logic would be nice
    It's even clear to Fred
He doesn't take his own advice,
    He takes the plunge instead.

Consoling him for such a lapse
    We tell him that we think:
His lore may be of use to chaps
    Who totter on the brink.

But Fred can't stand the ruck at all
    Who look before they leap.
What's more they're just the ones who call
    His 'cynicism' cheap.

Fred Puts the Clock Back

Fred muses on those eras when
  A woman would 'confer
Her favours on' some lucky man
  And *he* would 'pleasure' *her*.

'Have sex with', 'have it off with' – this
  Jargon gives no sense
Of all those warm benignities,
  That sweet beneficence.

UNDERTONES AND OVERTONES

Fred, Film Critic

"Explicit Sex": Fred says that means,
  In cinematic terms,
Humans set in carnal scenes
  Like pekes or pachyderms.

Nothing's less like the act of love,
  As those inside it feel,
Than such a representation of
  Its semblance on a reel:

On filming how a couple screws,
  With camera panned up close,
"Silly"'s a word that one might use –
  Another one is "gross".

So, round by round and blow by blow
  With false or faulty touch,
Their lenses' scope can only show
  Too little or too much.

Some erotica Fred's known
  – Exceptional, it's true –
(Indian, for instance) has a tone
  Truthful and tender too.

But, on film the whole thing (which
  Sometimes has occurred)
Can only reach us real and rich
  If adequately blurred.

While Fred hates in the average show
  Intrusive action by
The male partner ... and no,
  He can't "identify".

Even the pure, romantic screen
  Never exactly charms
Old Fred, with some young honey queen
  In someone else's arms.

Fred Fills One in

Check one: Success ☐; Health ☐; Feeling free ☐;
   Fully requited love ☐;
Your chance of immortality ☐;
   Or none of the above ☐.

Fred's answer? – Well, it seems (though some
   Would take it to denote
A mind unsalvageably dumb)
   Love still might get his ☒.

Fred and the Founding Fathers

By 'prejudice' we understand
  A blend of common-sense:
The wisdom of the ages and
  Life's experience.

Similarly with 'stereotyped',
  Much used by trendies when
They want all knowledge quite wiped
  Out – then start again.

A base camp in that hard-won lore
  Serves Fred and others who
May move out from it to explore
  Whatever's strange and new.

Fred the Healer

Fred doesn't harp on it a lot
  And yet this thought persists:
There can't be many men who're not
  Part-time misogynists.

So he's devised this therapy
  To make the strain grow less,
Such feelings abreacted by
  Being brought to consciousness.

X X X Fred

Some find – what may unman the best –
   Although she freely strips,
A girl, quite lavish of the rest,
   A prude about her lips.

It puts in question, straight away,
   How far the union goes:
Mutual surrender, Fred would say,
   Must stretch from head to toes.

And when a couple's loins press tight,
   Locked in the act of love,
A formal handshake mayn't seem right
   To link the parts above.

That's why not only Fred – for this
   Applies to lots of males –
May find that if denied a kiss
   Their whole performance fails.

Fred and Fable

Some chaps are like the fabled frogs:
　　They get, when they re-wed
In a reaction from Queen Log's
　　Regime, Queen Stork's instead.

Who knows what Aesop had in mind:
　　But politics of strife
Or compromise are not confined
　　Only to public life.

Fred and Fifi

Old Fred's imagination has
   In its conceptual net
A honey whom he thinks of as
   Fifi Lafolette.

French maid, or can-can dancer at
   Folies or Moulin Rouge,
She may best serve to indicate
   A really not too huge

Array of varied images
   In vision's repertoire,
Exotic with her flashing eyes
   And her unfloating hair:

One of a princely harem? Well,
   For accuracy's sake
Let's say, of the material
   From which a lad can make

A sort of sensual symphony
   (Blonde Swede, Circassian slave ...
Sometimes a mix of two or three,
   At most of four or five).

A film across reality?
   A meld of metaphors?
A symbol of humanity?
   A condiment or sauce? ...

When actual girls come into play
   The tactful little pet
Just waves her hand and trips away.
   (Her perfume lingers yet.)

Fred and the Double Standard

A double standard? Fred would say
    (In confidence): well, yes,
The universe is built that way
    Which one can't second-guess.

They win, say, three times out of five
    (Some chaps would make it four):
A truly just alternative
    Would hardly give them more.

And while a woman never doubts
    (As Fred observes these things)
Her losses on the roundabouts
    She just forgets the swings.

But Fred won't openly apply
    This test of them and us:
To raise the double standard high
    Provokes a fearsome fuss.

Fred Investigates

Do chaps find life with ones that scold
   Worse than with ones that sulk?
Well, of the sample Fred has polled
   The answer is, the bulk

Just vote against the mode from which
   Their present sufferings stem
("Don't Knows" have pasts containing each
   But now are shot of them.)

"These weighted questions," experts prate,
   "That ill-constructed curve ..."
But Gallup won't co-operate
   So Fred's will have to serve.

Fred Faces Facts

If *Blanc de Blancs* and *Blanc de Noirs*
  (Fred muses, rather pissed)
Are possible, as most things are,
  Can *Noir de Blancs* exist?

His reason tells him in a tick
  This is the merest dream.
But is his intellect so quick
  When women are the theme?

Not without effort. For he'll let
  His fantasy grow fond
Of, let us say, a blonde brunette
  (A sort of *Brune de Blondes*),

With eyes of blackly hazel-blue
  And skin all ivory-tanned;
Tall, tiny; slim and buxom too;
  Huge breasts that fit the hand.

– Such dreams he can return to store
  (Albeit with regret),
But others come which lure chaps more
  Insidiously yet:

A temperamental and serene
  Bohemian home-girl type;
A *poule de luxe* of modest mien,
  Mature and not yet ripe;

Demure, farouche; unspoilt and chic ...
  Of course the lesson is
He shouldn't actually seek
  For contradictories.

So when he toasts a girl in *Brut*,
  From Ay or Avise slopes,
Fred take the realistic view
  – Or so he says he hopes.

Footnote

    Girls aren't exempt. Their dreams evoke
      (Fred hears it every day)
    The strong and independent bloke
      Who'll do just what they say.

Fred and the Frigid

Some girls, from stuff they've heard or read,
  Embracing, think they must
Dig their long nails right into Fred
  To prove untrammeled lust.

Old Fred's recourse, such as it is
  – Just cease all movement till
They've ended such barbarities,
  Then work your mutual will.

But even odder female lore
  Fred's heard of, though he's missed,
Is girls who think a man gets more
  Excited if their fist

At the most sexy moment claps
  An ice-cube to his . . . Oh
Think of the suffering that chaps
  Go through that we don't know!

Fred's back soon heals. But when he'd see
  Things like the ice-cube hoax,
He'd long mourn girls' credulity
  At some sod's heartless jokes.

Fred and the *Ars Amatoria*

Of course Fred's read the *Art of Love*
   But Ovid always seems
(To him at least) the picture of
   A cynic sunk in schemes.

Fred finds the whole approach unsound,
   As tasteless as it's trite,
Though he concedes a cynic's bound
   To get a few things right.

Fred on Fascism

"Fascism is," a learned don
   Once told Fred in a bar,
"A feminine phenomenon."
   Fred wouldn't go so far.

The phrase might sound, Fred would admit,
   Felicitous and fine;
The chap was perhaps too struck with it:
   Where should one draw the line?

"The ruthless certainty they're right ...
   Such parallels are plain.
And yet their tactics are not quite
   As easy to contain."

"And when our lads, who'd laid it low
   In Berlin and in Rome,
Marched back they found it wasn't so
   Simple a task at home ..."

Watching him stagger off, Fred thought
   Only in academe
Does one find such a fancy sort
   Of way to blow off steam.

Fred Outflanked

Our mores, so Fred used to feel,
 Should just be strict enough
That less than his own sex-appeal
 Would not tempt girls to love.

The competition thus cut down ...
 But soon he found, of course,
Girls so mad keen on clod or clown
 This logic lost its force.

Footnotes from Fred

1.

"Si la jeunesse savait, si
  La Viellesse pouvait", yet
Fred brings up an anomaly
  That aphorists forget.

He finds that, with the years he's spanned,
  In his not special case,
The savvy's finally to hand,
  The pouvy still in place.

2.

Of course, the knowledge has its gaps,
  The power sometimes fails,
And, as with all imperfect chaps,
  Incompetence prevails.

In any case, he'd hardly claim
  That spoilsports like La Roche-
foucauld would ever mark his name
  "Sans peur et sans reproche."

Fred Seeks Guidance

Philosophers might help? Although
  Fred sees they mainly stick
To how we know the things we know,
  What makes the cosmos tick.

There could be good stuff all the same
  In some old sage or seer,
And Epicurus seemed a name
  That might make all things clear.

Well, that old seeker after truth
  Said prudent chaps had best
Avoid the "fine, exciting, smooth
  Movements" of thigh and breast.

And what's the good of that to Fred?
  – Or Plato's two-backed beast?
Impatiently he shakes his head
  And tries the mystic East.

But they just tell him He and She
  Are merely Yang and Yin
Implying total symmetry ...
  Well, one can only grin.

In some ways Fred's a bit naive,
  It seems to be his fate
To take what deeper thinkers leave
  And try to set it straight.

Hurrah for Hume and Locke and Hobbes!
  And yet, when all is said,
– Except from intellectual snobs –
  A brief hurrah for Fred!

SOONER AND LATER

Fail-safe Fred

Some people think, though it's not true,
    Fred's nature is inclined
To take too sceptical a view
    Of love and womankind.

Addiction to the other sex
    Is praised, and shared, by Fred,
He just thinks there are side-effects
    On which light should be shed.

And though explorers can't be safe
    There's one rule they should keep:
Don't use a leaky bathyscape
    To probe the dangerous deep.

Fred and Fats

"Your feet's too big!" Fats Waller sings
　　As Fred turns on the tape
And wonders why supernal things
　　Depend on women's shape.

They do, though, don't they? Still, it's crude
　　Put in this Waller way:
Fred plays, in a more highbrow mood,
　　"La donna è mobile"

But belts out Waller's words (no prig
　　Or purist he): the pause
He puts before "your feet's too big"
　　And after "hates ya 'cause".

This sort of melds, so Fred would say,
　　Their physique and their mind;
Both, this time, in a tasteless way,
　　Still, he might try to find

– For the same treatment – tunes on those
　　Whose temperaments are sweet,
And bodies fine down to the toes
　　Of pretty little feet.

Fred on Feedback

Girls look prettiest when they're sweet
  Entailing the reverse:
That when they know they're looking beat
  They start behaving worse.

Fred's read some cybernetic stuff
  – With systems acting so
Even in principle it's tough
  To stabilize the flow.

Not that he has to turn to books,
  Or scan the printed page,
Never to tell one that she looks
  Appalling in a rage.

Dear Fred

Fred's boasted to us once or twice
   And only half in jest,
That were there columns of advice
   For men, his would be best.

One of the problems that arise:
   If you've contrived to poach
A party girl, and there she lies,
   Her eyes crammed with reproach,

When you – perhaps because of horm-
   one shortage, psychic block –
Have been unable to perform:
   There's shame, and even shock.

Fred would advise you thus: Don't say
   "It's not occurred before,
I don't know what went wrong today,"
   Upsetting her still more.

Don't say "I've had too many drinks,"
   Don't blame a lack of nerve.
(Being let down once or twice, Fred thinks,
   Is what we all deserve.)

But hang your head, and say "My dear,
   You have such lovely eyes!
This happens all the time, I fear,
   I do apologise!"

And if the rumour gets around,
   As well the rumour might,
Then some advantage can be found:
   A girl may stay the night.

– "I feel so safe with (let's say) Fred"
  Yet get a nice surprise
When things build up a storm instead
  – What kudos that implies!

So any parfit, gentle guy
  Should bear the point in mind
(While more concerned with courtesy
  Than smugness at being "kind").

Fred Tries to Help

When a friend of Fred's obsessed
　With some quite ghastly girl,
Fred takes him lunching at a rest-
　aurant, where thoughts of her'll

Lose some allure. It's slickly posh
　With female clientele:
The carrots' crunch, the yoghourt's slosh,
　The chintzy drinks they sell.

Tiny glass tables glint too bright
　From pit and mezzanine,
At one of them he sits cramped tight.
　But heard is worse than seen:

Across the lettuces and leeks
　Which dreadful dressings souse,
Echo the chattering, the shrill shrieks,
　As in the Parrot House.

Aversion therapy, in fact.
　Is it of much avail?
Fred thinks that in one case he tracked
　It seemed to turn the scale.

Fred on Literature

A "woman's magazine" is where
  Yeasty emotions rise
And thwarted love and hearts' despair
  Grip throats and soften eyes.

A "girlie" magazine's effect
  Is, on the other hand,
With methods rather more direct
  To give old Fred a stand.

Women may shake their heads in scorn:
  How low can our lot get?
While Fred just thinks how overdrawn
  Those wet romances; yet

Still grants her vision's higher tone
  While staring himself blind.
A difference – not the only one –
  Between two types of mind.

Fred Gives Up

On marriage, Fred has things to tell
   Culled from many a friend
– But is it all reliable?
   And whither does it tend?

One pair on which Fred thought he'd check
   Had won the Dunmow Flitch:
The husband was a trembling wreck,
   The wife a raving bitch.

One pair was prone to public rage:
   Outside their house one day
Fred listened as they seemed to stage
   A sentimental play.

Marriage is such a strange affair
   That no one really knows
– Not even Fred – how any pair
   Stack up the cons and pros.

Festive Fred

De minimis non curat Fred,
   Or so he'll often boast,
But some things send him off his head
   That don't loom large to most.

Christmas comes but once a year
   And as to what it means
To Fred, he's often made it clear
   He sees two different scenes:

The first is when at Christmastide
   And not engaged or wed,
Girls go back to their parents' side
   And leave a lonesome Fred

Who, with stout, claret, whiskey, hock,
   With Melton Mowbray pies,
With tins of tasty tongue in stock,
   Stretched on his sofa lies.

He doesn't shave. He reads a lot.
   Soft jazz relieves the hush.
He hugs himself to think he's not
   Out in the sleet and slush.

Holed up in his basement flat,
   Such simple joys suffice:
The thought of all the mishaps that
   He's missing adds the spice.

Viz: Christmas trees, charades, church – this
   All taking place amid
A rat-faced brother talking piss,
   An ankle-kicking kid;

And worse! – Some solace, as he can't
　　Deny, may perhaps be found:
A bright and bodice-bursting aunt,
　　A sympathetic hound.

Fred's fair, so mentions this relief
　　But adds that, truth to tell,
Such interludes are rare, and brief,
　　And all the rest is hell.

He daren't drink suitably. Instead
　　His brain gets out of phase,
He doesn't follow half that's said
　　He drags round in a daze ...

Weeks or months, you'd think to hear
　　Old Fred, are thus misspent
Instead of just three days a year
　　– Not even one percent!

Which a less fine-bred chap might stand
　　(Except when matters seem
So balanced that a grain of sand
　　Would make them kick the beam).

Fred For the Defence

"My wife's a bourgeois philistine,"
  A lefty said to Fred,
Fred stopped him: chaps who take this line
  Make him see fairly red.

This was a girl it chanced he knew:
  No lowbrow Tory but
Bohemian, intellectual too,
  And merely not a slut.

Fred on Feminism

On Women's Rights – what should one say?
  Does Fred have any tips?
Fred's usual answer is to lay
  His finger to his lips.

Pressed further – here there's no safe line,
  It's bound to leave you limp;
Object, and you're a macho swine,
  Enthuse, and you're a wimp.

"Of course, in general I agree"
  Is used by cagey chaps;
But can you stand the strain as she
  Looks out for any lapse?

The best (which isn't very good)
  Start off with "What the hell!"
Then say, at last you've understood,
  She puts it all so well.

Better seek other subjects of
  Which couples may converse:
Her beauty, soccer, Larkin, love
  – At least none could be worse.

Fred Looks Back

Fred's lived through various epochs and
  Having no patience with
False retrospect, he takes the stand
  That contrary to myth

The Sixties weren't much good for sex:
  In order to play fair
Good-looking girls wore hideous specs
  And grew long greasy hair.

Fred grants "sex" happened, even that
  Its quantity increased,
But plates piled high with mutton fat
  Don't make a gourmet feast.

Fred Gets It Wrong

Oh no, we never mention her.
   – Because her name might make
Such hellish images recur
   As even Fred can't take?

For once your guess would turn out wrong:
   This time the problem is
Not letting Fred go on too long
   With happy memories.

She was his secretary, and more;
   And so they went away
To take off March and April for
   A working holiday.

A peasant hut, fixed by a friend:
   From nine Fred would dictate
While she took shorthand and got tanned.
   (As Fred's now keen to state,

Such work together may enrich
   Vacant vacation days
To a good intimacy which
   You miss if you just laze.)

Then, sour wine and canned corned beef
   And next, an icy swim
From the sea-urchin-studded reef:
   It all seemed fine to him.

A stroll down to the little port,
   A trudge the two miles back
Heavy with provender they'd bought
   Between them in a sack.

Fred Gets It Wrong

At dusk she'd do the typing up
  While Fred set to and strove
To stew the stuff on which they'd sup
  Upon the butane stove.

And so to bed. It seemed to him
  The soft play of desire
Sank through a salt-aired sleep to brim
  Contentment each day higher.

Then home. The recent victim of
  A marital affray,
So still too numb to mention love,
  Fred let her get away.

Was she a rose without a thorn?
  Fred asks as one of those
Who's more than once been scratched and torn
  By thorns without a rose.

And if they'd wed? Though Fred will say
  Well, thorns are bound to sprout,
And petals fade and fall away,
  One sees he's still in doubt.

Fred at a Wedding

Fred's been to marriages before
  (Though mostly to his own).
He stifles, if perhaps no more
  Than other chaps, a groan

At tedium, cramp, a shirt too tight ...
  But shudders as he spies
The awful air of triumph bright
  In all the female eyes.

And his discomfort grows profound
  As if he had to view
A lot of lionesses round
  A poor sod of a gnu.

Fred Has Faith

"The right true end of love" said Donne,
　　Is taking girls to bed,
And now three centuries have gone
　　He's seconded by Fred.

Dean of St. Paul's? – Not when he wrote.
　　But many a modern Dean
Writes stuff on sex Fred wouldn't quote
　　(So soppy and obscene).

Et Fred in Arcadia

The sort of life Fred tends to lead
    May seem to suit him, but
Sometimes, he'll readily concede
    It drives him off his nut.

And when he turns to metaphor,
    He puts it that he hacks
His way through thorny jungles or
    Up icy mountain tracks.

Of course he'd grant that this is how
    To gain experience:
– He's had enough of that for now:
    A break would make some sense ...

So, more than once in his career,
    Fred's copped right out and spent
(As other chaps might) half a year
    In unrelieved content,

Preferably in rural shacks
    With just a bit of ground,
Where he can work and then relax
    With hobby, hearth and hound

– A basset (say), its muzzle on
    His knee – he swigs (say) Scotch
Curled up contentedly to con
    (Say) *How to Mend a Watch*.

Drip-dry shirts, washed in the shower,
    Booze chosen to his whim,
Shaved when he liked, bed at an hour
    That simply suited *him*.

Celibacy? Not quite. He'd seek
    For the odd far-off peach
For just the odd weekend or week
    In travel or on beach.

She goes. The parting's bitter-sweet
    – A savour that goes well
With '62 Château Lafite
    And *Veau aux Chanterelles*.

(He tells himself the point with pith
    Until he gets it plain:
His house can't be his castle with
    A live-in chatelaine.)

But these brief cats-paws scarcely stir
    The millpond of his mind,
No nightmare memories recur:
    Those scenes are left behind.

And when he starts to find the pace
    Too slow, and summer fails,
His stamina's built up to face
    The equinoctial gales.

Fred Counts the Ways

Sometimes sex is glorious fun,
   And sometimes sweet delight,
Dark deeps dissolving them to one,
   A sort of feral fight.

In some moods Fred will make it more
   And talk of five or six
Such options. But he'd settle for
   The second (or a mix).

In Conclusion

Fred at the Finish

Fred *is* of service to his kind,
   Or so we all must hope,
And those should bear his points in mind
   Who plan to (say) elope.

His views are quite consistent (but
   He'd plead a change of mood).
His touch, though sometimes delicate,
   More often's pretty crude.

But if his warnings sound too stark
   It's only thus one schools
Chaps who might otherwise embark
   Upon a Ship of Fools.

He doesn't always come out well
   From stuff that he relates:
– He waives his self-conceit to tell
   What may affect their fates.

The good things about girls, Fred says,
   Are clear to all who've looked:
He could go on like that for days
   – They really have him hooked.

He's lots of evidence to prove
   Only with them you'd find
Such lovingness when they're in love
   Such kindness when they're kind.

And if the tributes thus bestowed
   Are seldom here expressed,
It's that they fit a lyric mode
   That other chaps do best.

Though most men hope, if perhaps not soon,
   Eventually to lie
At anchor in the blue lagoon,
   Their chances don't seem high.

Mourning all those who've come to grief
   On stormy seas of sex,
He seeks a passage through the reef
   Guided by previous wrecks.

A Note About Robert Conquest

Robert Conquest was born in Malvern, Worcestershire, in 1917, to an American father and his English wife. Educated at Winchester College, the University of Grenoble, and Magdalen College, Oxford, he took his B.A. and (later) M.A. degrees in politics, philosophy, and economics, and his D. Litt. in Soviet history.

In Lisbon on an American passport at the outbreak of the Second World War, he returned to England to serve in the Oxfordshire and Buckinghamshire Light Infantry, and in 1944 was sent from Italy on Balkan military missions awkwardly attached to the Soviet Third Ukrainian Front – and later the Allied Control Commission in Bulgaria. From 1946 to 1956, he worked in the British Foreign Service – first in Sofia, then in London, and in the U.K. Delegation to the United Nations – after which he varied periods of freelance writing with academic appointments.

Conquest's poems were published in various periodicals from 1937. In 1945 the PEN Brazil Prize for a war poem was awarded to his "For the Death of a Poet" – about an army friend, the poet Drummond Allison, killed in Italy (published in *The Book of the PEN 1950*) – and in 1951 he received a Festival of Britain verse prize. Since then he has brought out seven volumes of poetry previous to *Blokelore & Blokesongs*, and one of literary criticism (*The Abomination of Moab*). He has published a verse translation of Aleksandr Solzhenitsyn's epic *Prussian Nights* (1977), and two novels, *A World of Difference* (1955), and (with Kingsley Amis) *The Egyptologists* (1965). In 1955 and 1963 Conquest edited the influential *New Lines* anthologies, and in 1962-1963 he was literary editor of the *London Spectator*.

He is the author of twenty-one books on Soviet history, political philosophy, and international affairs, the most recent being *The Dragons of Expectation* (2004). His classic, *The Great Terror*, has appeared in most European languages, as well as in Japanese, Arabic, Hebrew and Turkish.

In 1959-60 he was Visiting Poet and Lecturer in English at the University of Buffalo, and has also held research appointments at the London School of Economics, the Columbia University Russian Institute, the Woodrow Wilson International Center for Scholars, the Heritage Foundation, and Harvard University's Ukrainian Research Institute.

In 1990 he presented Granada Television's *Red Empire*, a seven-part documentary on the Soviet Union which was broadcast in the UK, the USA, and in various other countries, including Australia and Russia.

Conquest is a Fellow of the British Academy, the American Academy of Arts and Sciences, the Royal Society of Literature, and the British Interplanetary Society; he is also a member of the Society for the Promotion of Roman Studies (contributing to *Britannia* an article on the Roman Place Names of Scotland). His honours and awards include the Presidential Medal of Freedom; the Companion of the Order of St. Michael and St. George; the Order of the British Empire; the Commander Cross of the Order of Merit of the Republic of Poland; the Ukrainian Order of Yaroslav Mudryi; the Estonian Cross of Terra Mariana Order of Merit; the Jefferson Lectureship; the American Academy of Arts and Letters' Michael Braude Award for Light Verse; the Richard Weaver Award for Scholarly Letters; and the Fondazione Liberal Career Award.

He and his wife Elizabeth live in California, where he has long worked as a research fellow at Stanford University's Hoover Institution.

Other books from Waywiser

Other Books from Waywiser